salmonpoetry

Diverse Voices from Ireland and the World

Blackfish

ELVIS ALVES

3/26/22

Dear Michael,
Great meeting you at AWP
Philadelphia. Here are words
culled from life. May you

continue on your journey

with success.

Warmly,

Published in 2022 by
Salmon Poetry
Cliffs of Moher, County Clare, Ireland
Website: www.salmonpoetry.com
Email: info@salmonpoetry.com

Copyright © Elvis Alves, 2022

ISBN 978-1-915022-10-3

Cover Image: *???*
Cover Design & Typesetting: *Siobhán Hutson*

Printed in Ireland by Sprint Print

For My Nephews

CONTENTS

Blackfish

Espina

Sushi

Ichthys

But I smell some of the smoke of Babylon on I. Come closer. Closer.

—Rowan Ricardo Phillips
Purgatorio, XXVI: 135-148.

Blackfish

Balance

Absent is the medicine capable of stilling the beast. That
lies within and among a forest of souls. Quaking with fear
of toppling.

All must come to an end. Life is the will
to live beyond eternity.

A task doomed to fail before it is thought of
or attempted. And carries a fate written on ash-shaven heads.
Foretelling a future that will never come.

What really matters lives in the now. Like the power of dreams
destroyed by the hands of reality. Or the joy that flees simply because it can.

That is why there is the call for an experience more lasting than the last. More
tantalizing than the first. And is void of beginning and end.

A Knee in the Heart

My father told me how to defend myself as a child.
He said that I should hit the attacker on the knee—hard—
that this would disable him.

My father never told me how to prevent a heartbreak
or how to heal from one.

I wonder why he did not teach me this lesson.
Is a broken knee more important to him than a broken heart?

No. 01

This is what I am called
when you call me to
come to you

&

I flee from you;
wanting to go somewhere
else but not knowing where.

Life is a destination
unknown.

Go.

On Visit to Hellshire Beach (Jamaica)

He cleans fish where water touches steps of stone leading
to dry land and mouth of makeshift shack where man with

stained apron fries fish in large pan of oil on top of stove
fueled by burning wood, and serves it with bammie.

The smell of frying fish, sound of oil jumping in pan, do not
distract from the itinerant fishmonger with scars like roadways

on bone-thin face, and knife in dexterous hands shedding scales
from fish, scales that swim in air like dust disturbed by strong wind,

some return to the ocean, others scatter like loosed pearls at my feet.
"My father did this to me," the man says, without removing knife from fish.

I said to him, "Daddy, I am your son. You gonna kill me?"

I imagine he has told the story many times before, and shares it with
me because not everyone escapes an attempt of untimely death.

That Dog My Father Killed

I was seven when my father returned
from 'merica—to visit us

and bring with him the weight that comes with eating
cheap food in long winters,

and the supposed strength this weight gives.

I watched as he lifted stones and threw them
at a running dog.

Each pelt hitting its target.
Each stone heavier than the one before.

I heard the yelps of the dog and was surprised because
until then, I did not know all animals carried language.

Sport over, I watch my father and a neighbor dump
the dog in a river.

I imagined the fishes feasting on the dog but not before
surrounding it as if a halo.

Reggaemylitist

(for Peter Tosh)

Amalgamation of
joy & pain.

A raised machete that
strikes with care.

Lyrical movement that
moves with beats,
spells relief.

Born in Africa,
reincarnated in Jamaica.

Sound of feet stomping on
grave of Ba-be-wrong.

Feel of a woman's waist;
a sensual embrace.

Tuff love.

Meal with appeal and
everything in-between.

Amongst my African Brothers in New York City

(for the Ojevwe brothers)

Oh brothers, did the blue of the Caribbean and white
winters of New York serve to wash me clean of you?

We dance separate rhythms. We eat different foods.

I am ashamed to say but it is a fact that spaghetti and
meatballs, cold cut sandwiches, and pierogis, yes, even

pierogis, agree with my stomach more than your native
peppa soup with goat meat, suya chicken, and roasted

banana eaten with peanuts. Oh brothers, must my stomach,
like my mind, too, be decolonized? If yes, where is the Chef

Fanon? Oh brothers, is my love for you not enough?

No. 1979

"After all, you are a man," the woman says to me in an accent thick like mascara on the face of a girl who thinks she is not pretty enough.

I had mistakenly jumped ahead of her, preoccupied with wanting to buy a stamp before the parking enforcement officer ticked my car parked in front of the post office.

I had refused to put money in the meter, thinking I could get away with the minor offense.

"Sorry. Go ahead," I said to the woman, after I realized what I had done. She did not budge. The hands that fed her nonsense held her still.

Fat Boy

The words he spoke sounded
familiar because he said them

before when I was a boy
and I wanted to hear anything

other than what he said and tonight,

my father told me what he said then
when I was a boy.

"You gained weight. A lot."

Now I am grown, and the words
he said then hurt the same now.

He did not quantify what
a lot is. I am not and have

never been obese. In writing this
poem, I realize my father spoke

nonsense to me when I was a
boy and he continues to speak

nonsense now that I am grown and
he is getting old, losing his hair—going

bald and crazy. How else to explain
a man calling his son fat, not using

concise words, not caring how the
son would react? So I write this

poem not to recite the nonsense of
my father but to bury it with words.

Monk

(for Thelonious Monk)

I

Thelonious's fingers have holes.
They smell of something sweetly fetid,
and tell of life gone awry or of an omen on the
horizon.

II

A man walks into a bar and hears Thelonious playing
the piano. He pulls out a gun and fires at the piano
and player. Thelonious keeps playing, with holes in
fingers.

III

Do you play? Yes. What? Jazz.
That's the Devil's music.

IV

Blood everywhere. The assailant gets away
but a police officer catches up to him few
blocks from the scene. He confesses to attempted
murder of music and some guy named Monk.

V

Thelonious speaks: "Yeah, right, blood was everywhere.
But these fingers are made of something special.
Nothing can kill 'em, not even God himself."

My Mother Cried the Night She Fell
Out of Love with Karl Malone

Karl Malone was a power forward on the good ol' Utah Jazz.
He held his own on the basketball court, as if he was born to

throw ball through net. He cradled it with hands of thunder. Lightning
struck when he dunked it. Karl Malone's greatest asset

was his smile. It made my mother melt. When time for a foul shot,
he walked to the free throw line like a rooster with mountains for

chest. He would wink at the camera and smile. That was when my
mother melted. She believed the wink and smile were for her.

Then it happened; a television interview unraveled the love affair. It
was not what Karl Malone said, but what he did or did not do that

offended my mother. When I heard my mother crying, I rushed into the
room, kissed her on the cheeks, and used my hands to dry her tears.

I followed her eyes to the television screen and saw what she was looking at.
Two of the children sat up front, Karl Malone and his white wife in the center.

Behind them, to the left, was the third child. A boy. His phenotype proved that
he was not born of them. Late into the night, and days after the interview, I argued

Karl Malone's case. Surely it was a mistake, like placing an a where an
e belongs in independence. My argument did not persuade my mother to forgive

Karl Malone. She charged him with the only sin a mother cannot forgive: not loving
his child.

Blackfish

Rules and Regulations:

• The Department of Environmental Protection Agency states a LIMIT of 4 Blackfish (Tautoga Onitas) 16 inches or longer to be removed from the Erie Basin per day per person.

• All Blackfish (Tautoga Onitas) under 16 inches long must be returned to the Erie Basin waters.

I

I do not want to be a blackfish
plucked from my home, prodded
and returned maimed, or killed and
eaten.

II

I do not want to die like Jesus
crowned with thorns, mocked,
and nailed to a cross to die a
slow death, while the captors
divide my clothes below.

III

I, at Gethsemane:

Admonish Peter for failing to decapitate
the Roman soldier, cutting off
his ear instead.

Take sword and do the job myself.
Hold bloody head in hand while swinging
sword at Judas's head, kill him

and the soldiers that came with him.
March the survivors to the edge of a spiked
cliff and watch as they fall like
the dirty swine they are.

IV

If I must die, let it be for freedom,
nothing less. But let me die fighting back.

Fishmonger's Prayer Gets Answered

Dear Fish, give us our daily
bread so that we can invest it
far from here and let these people
fry their fish because they would
need to buy oil and high sodium
fish-fry mix also available at the fish
market. Salmon.

Conversation at the fish market: mother and son.

These Korean muthafuckas are making mad bread up in
here by selling these rotten ass muthafucking fish.

Shut your muthafucking dirty mouth. Where did you learn
to curse like that?

I don't like fish. I want to eat chicken. Let's eat at
Kentucky Fried Chicken, Popeyes Fried Chicken,
Kennedy Fried Chicken.

Boy, we ain't eating at none of those restaurants.
The only place we going after here is Long John's
Liquor Store 'cross the street.

Walking out the fish market, with plastic bags
of fillets of whiting, porgy, two heads of farm-raised
salmon, and bottle of oil and box of fish-fry mix, mother
and child are met by Reverend Calvin Klein, of the Fish-
Baptized Holiness Church, and choir, protesting violence
against fish, singing we shall overcome some day.

Someday My Prince Will Come

(for Trayvon Martin)

Until then let us sing a song and
pray to the heavens within that the
evil among us will not triumph.

Sleep, sweet innocence.
Death's ring on your throat.
There's a day when all will be free
and eyes see what is to be.

This morning my heart woke with
sorrow, broken by a force unknown
but felt and powerful to the blow.

This too will pass. My people have
come a long way. We carry the dead
with us.

The truth cannot be buried.
It lives. It is alive.

We are waiting for the sound of
the abeng, a charge led by a prince.

Espina

Merchant of Stones

I come, a merchant of stones

begging you to pick up and throw
them at the lies you tell yourself,

until they die and you live like one
who reaches Nirvana.

Eschatology

It won't be fun.
It won't be fun.

Children, who are you
worshipping?

Rise mighty warriors and
take your posts.

Armageddon is on the
opposite shore.

It's the great gettin' up
morning.

Day has turned to night.

The birds have flown to
God knows where.

It won't be fun.
It won't be fun.

Rise mighty warriors
and take your posts.

Gather your swords
from ploughshares.

The enemies are approaching
across the way.

Rise mighty warriors
for day has turned to
night.

Old women refuse
to pray.

Children are pregnant
with hunger.

And decay is everywhere.

Oh children, who are
you worshipping?
Oh children, can't you
see that day has turned
to night?

Epiphany

I am happy to be the one who can walk and talk with the sky, a platter
of gold coins raining on my golden head, no longer made of clay.

And then it hits me like music; this thing called life hits me and
I cannot do otherwise but dance.

Dance in tune, dance out of tune.

Move hips, hands, feet in whatever orders or angles, move to
the beat that keeps hitting me.

I cannot help but be carried over the gates that open the soul to a
world not found until this moment when I realize that what I have

been waiting for will never come because it is present and
simply awaits discovery, to be seen by eyes that looked everywhere

but at the gift—even though dressed with flowers and adorned with
bow as blue as the sky, standing still drinking the ocean's water

that gives life to every creeping thing on earth. An earth that revolves
and grows with the beating of my heart.

Black Moses

The man with chain on neck
crosses my path.

"Black Moses," he says and walks
away.

I follow him, and chain.

He turns left.
Then left again,

back to where we
started.

"Black Moses," he says,
and walks away.

I follow him.

But this time yell,
"set thy people free!"

He stops, looks at me,
picks up the chain,

and tosses it at me.

It turns to a ball of fire.
         Deep in my soul.
         Deep in my soul.

"Black Moses," he says,
and walks away.

Black Jesus

Where is my black Jesus? His hands of fire on my head in the day.
His feet black pearls walking through my dreams at night.

Tell me, my black Jesus, whose son are you?

Send a message to me that I will live.
Reveal the ladder used to descend the heavens

unfurling beneath this pen where all animals but
humans roam in peace.

Black is the Color of My Hair (or My Experience at a Quaker Meeting)

I'm turning into a specter before your very eyes and I'm going to haunt you.

-Jean Genet, *The Blacks: A Clown Show*

I was thinking of you,
(Who are you?)

when we were in the Meeting House.
(Why are you here?)

Why were you thinking of me?

Because Quakerism must be new
to you.
(I'm still trying to figure out why you are here.)

Actually, this is my second stint teaching
at a Quaker School.

     (...Oh.)

The Procrastinator

(for Lee Morgan)

Lee does not come around anymore.
Got too big for us.
He plays uptown, at clubs where people
with money go for good drinks and good
music.

But, I'll tell you this, good music lives
where the poor lives.
A man has to dig deep in his soul to
create music that shakes the world.

That was what Lee did when he made
The Procrastinator.

He dug deep inside and pulled with
might a song big as the fish that swallowed
Jonah whole.

That was then.
This is now.

He ain't the same.
Money and women got to him.
I know they are not the same but
each can make a man go insane.

Lee's gone.
He's not coming home.
Tried to take music with him
but she lives in these alleyways with
the poor.

There is something about survival that not
every man understands because to survive
is to know that you are close to death
and death, my friend, is no
procrastinator.

No.23

The parents have eaten sour grapes, and the children's teeth are set on edge.

(JEREMIAH 31:29)

I

There is no plant in the garden of my father's life whose
name I can call my own. What semblance lies between us
I see from afar. There is the dream my father tells:

> As a boy I wanted to be a journalist,
> travel the world,
> talk to people,
> and run with animals
> not housed in safaris.

Before my mother removed the T.V. from the living room,
my father would sit and watch the Discovery Channel for hours.
It was during these occasions he'd shared his dreams with us. He
shared little else.

He also played music. Soca, Calypso, and Black American R&B were
his favorites. Once, a classmate visited our home and heard Me & Mrs. Jones
for the first time.

His budding puberty budded with excitement, at hearing this anthem of adultery.
When he returned home, he called and asked if I could play Me & Mrs. Jones
and place the mouth of the telephone close to the radio.

I refused. I did not want to take the music away from my father.

II

My mother safeguards other people's children for a living. She has done this
since leaving Guyana as a young mother, bringing big dreams with her to
New York City.

White babies grow to love her more than they love their mothers.

Having no union to bargain wage, she takes the $15 per hour along with the extra week's pay every Christmas Holiday.

She refers to her employer as "my boss" and other than the white skin, I wonder who this nameless person is.

> Does she have a kind heart?
> What is the color of her hair?
> Does the color change when touched by light?
> Are her hands dipped in grace?
> Does she speak words coated with honey?
> Does she see my mother her slave?

Having pushed strollers along streets of DUMBO and lower Manhattan, my mother comes home too tired to cook, and complains of taking her charge to

> dance practices
> tutoring sessions
> swimming lessons
> doctor's appointments
> museum visits
> and more places
> and do more things
> and more
> and more
> …more
> for $15 per hour

When my mother washes the "boss's" laundry, does she see stains that prove love, too, lives in her house?

Vizcaya

When the Biscayne Bay opens its frothy mouth, everyone listens
including the American bourgeois who flock to Vizcaya to escape
the industrial smog they've manufactured.

At Vizcaya, the flowers bloom year round: dandelions greet tulips
which in turn kiss roses.

The vacationers are unlike the child who wakes after less than
three hours of sleep to walk through mountains of New England
snow to a factory with billowing smoke at its dome.

Smoke that spreads across the face of a choked sky, reaches Detroit,
Chicago, New York, and other cities inhabited by the poor, but

does not reach Vizcaya where the bourgeois sleep with rested feet
and dream of making money and of ways to increase their power.

They speak a language only greed can understand and which fails
to sooth the frost-bitten ears of the child walking mountains of snow
in homemade galoshes older than she is, and whose feet don't rest
even when she is dreaming.

Tragic Beauty

She wears weight
of world on
face.

But rolls away stones
from lips to reveal
a smile when she
sees me.

Sweet Fanta Diallo

(after Alpha Blondy)

Last time I saw her was at a psychiatric hospital.

Nothing alive in her eyes,
unable to recall my name,
life almost robbed from her.

Veins exposed on skin,
everything fading from
the girl I met in the city
and called like kin,

sweet Fanta Diallo.

We were classmates at
school. Like a fool, she
fell into my arms.

What good girl comes
to this city?

Sometimes we'd meet
on the hills. Without defense,
I conquered her with songs,
plant everything but a seed
inside of her.

That's why it was easy
to take everything and

leave nothing behind.

Sweet Fanta Diallo

She brings too many demons to bed with her,
and carries them like coins in purse, that
safeguard her body against my touch.

She does not touch me. Why don't you love me,
sweet Fanta Diallo? Am I ugly?

She confesses with a question: How can I
give you what was taken from me when I was
still a child?

Sweet Fanta Diallo

I know sweet Fanta Diallo.
I know her smile and the stories it tells.
Her laugh bursts with clouds.
Her tears, rain (not drops but torrent of water that
floods the ocean.) Trees sprout from her head.
Birds perch on their branches. I walk across
the bridge on her nose and witness suns rising
and falling in her eyes. There are roads on her
arms and legs. Her breasts are the tallest mountains.
I walk across her body, searching for and finding
nothing.

Samantha

(for John Edgar Wideman)

I

Matriarch of the Ark,
your womb an ocean from which
springs life beautiful and strong
as you are.

Samantha, mother to Junebug,
Becky, and others; Children who
love to fight and fight to love.

Take my hand, let us
dance and make another
with romance.

But this dream cannot come
true. You are locked away, not
in the Ark but at Mayview.

Your children, now grown,
scattered across the country-
Junebug lies beneath the ground,
mound of sorrow heaped
upon his crown.

This you know and that is
why you are where you are,
far—too far—from the ark,

white pills sitting on black
eyelids,

begging to be chewed and
swallowed like the grief that
holds you there—too far from
the Ark.

Grief that pulls down the
walls of the Ark, walls that
fall to pieces like stars at night
aborted by a careless sky.

Your children, once occupants
of the Ark, now run wild.

Run straight into drugs, violence,
and various forms of destruction
because you are no longer at its
helm.

II

But you—smart and gifted as you
are—have devised a plan to escape
Mayview, and take back what was
never given you: Peace of mind.

Somehow, some way, you will
get out of there,

and rebuild the Ark, stronger
than before, and gather your
children home.

Together, they will live in
peace and harmony.

Together, they will form
an army capable of fighting
evil.

III

Samantha at home,
calls her flock now
grown.

The Ark is rebuilt.

Spacious and safe, able
to hold the world in its
bosom.

Refuses to let evil in
even though it knocks
at the door.

Samantha is home.
It is the Fourth of July
and Junebug is alive.

Nothing really needs
restoring because everything
is the same, a circle that bends
but indeed remains a circle: Life.

Samantha is home, a place
she built with bare hands,
and populated with beautiful,
strong children spilling from her
womb,

reaching shores beyond the
native land.

They are all different, she says.

Sea. River. Ocean.

They are all different, but
meet and carry the Ark built
by the matriarch.

Nineveh

He uproots teeth primordial in nature.
And that eat his soul
with appetite the size of mercenary
forces plundering a city

whose inhabitants do not fight back,
because most are women,
children, and animals that
creep on all fours.

He knows of a city not spared and is
without name, unlike Nineveh,
whose repentant king decreed:

Human beings and animals shall be covered
with sackcloth, and they
shall cry mightily to God.

He thinks of what to do but knows he
is not the prophet Jonah
and therefore lives a life absent
of divine interventions.

Yet he wallows like Jonah when
swallowed by the whale of life.

A city stands in the far regions of his
soul, beckoning the presence
of creatures clothed with sackcloth.

Espina

The grocer sells salted Cod
and Haddock con espina,
sin espina.

Europeans rationed off salted
meat and fish to black slaves
in the Americas.

Colorful dilapidated restaurants
in my neighborhood serve up
bacalao along with salsa, merengue,
and bachata.

As for me, I wash clean the
salt from the fish—a task
impossible to do completely—

mix it with stir fry vegetables:
eggplant, spinach, bitter melon, squash.

The way my mother does it and
Her mother did it.

I trace my genealogy with food
and use the information to map
a route from the valley of dry bones.

Obeah Woman

(after Nina Simone)

I eat thunder.
Drink rain.
Hug the sun.
Call spirits and make them
run.

How do you think I lasted this long?

Dance with night.
Give birth to day.

Taste death—spit it out.
Rise with fire.
Grow with tree.
Run with river.

How do you think I lasted this long?

I am sister to my mother and mother
to my sister.

I sing the blues on top of tin
roof.

Scale the tallest mountain
without lifting a foot.

How do you think I lasted this long?

I make fools wise,
and the wise, fools.

Come close and die.
Come close and live.

If you stay far like a star,
shine bright.

Do right.
Don't quit.
Be quick.

You people from the islands
know what I am talking about.

My daughter says she does not get
those people.

I say to her, me too but I am fond
of 'em.

How do you think I lasted this long?

I live at the bottom of the ocean.
To get to Satan, you must pass
through me.

The angels answer my call.
I send them on missions with
the warning, "do no harm."

Sometimes they listen, sometimes
they don't.

I love them the same, without shame.

You are my children.
I love you the same,
without shame.

How do you think I lasted this long?

Sushi

Miles' Mood

(for Miles Davis)

Miles' mood is blue.
Sisyphillian.
Turmoil overload.
Horse with a heavy load.

Miles' mood carries
through walls thick with pain.

It soothes the beast within.

Miles' mood has heft, like a gun
has heft.
Like evil in the soul has heft.
Or, like bad news has heft.

Miles' mood is all bad.
Miles' mood is all good.

Miles' mood is life.

Inertia

Paginated by years
born unto death,
I lie on a bed of
sorrows.

Respite does not come.
I cannot eat my full.

Instead days pass,
leave me where
I lie contemplating
the inertia of being.

Three-Legged Buddha

(after the sculpture by Zhang Huan)

Dig a hole.
Put your head
in it.
Descartes was
wrong.
You are more
than a thought.

Doubt

Doubt is the tallest building
because therein lives
humanity.

Streets of St. Louis

Where a black body is left 4 ½ hours after the execution.
To show the people that this could happen to them, to you.

Especially if your skin is black. Like the gun that shot Mike
Brown down. Down in the ghetto. Down in the core of an America
without soul.

And therefore unable to save herself.

I beg you, dig me a hole to China. Or Africa. Where
there are more than a billion people strong to fight
the white man's oppression.

Men Drinking, Boys Tormenting, Dogs Barking

(after the painting by Bill Traylor)

That red line outlines where we can go. "Stay where you are,
boy, or else"...Pain. Death.

We do not believe in heaven because we are living in hell. Old
folks say that dogs bark after spirits. Barking dogs see what we
know, that the dead are not dead but haunt these parts like crime

committed in the dark. One boy told me that he did it just because
he could. The rest is not history but something absent from a book,
a tale told in the tormenting that is the now.

Reprieve comes in the warmth of a woman's touch but even that is
fleeting, like the liquor we drink and the days we dream would come
but never do.

Seizing

The victim's brain reaches limit in seconds, backfires
like an over-heated car engine.

Seizing, she lies where life attempts to end again and again.

Until the hand of time extinguishes internal sparks,
and causes here to cry,

"I peed myself"—sign of life.

Sushi

I cannot eat with sticks,
she says to me.

I watch as she stabs raw fish
with a metal fork.

For a woman whose taste is
catholic, I had expected otherwise.

Chinatown

Visit to Chinatown comes with invitation
to beheading. Roasted ducks, chickens, and pigs
hang headless on racks across broad windowpanes.

Before mounting steps to restaurant hidden between
office buildings like precious flower in a forest of tall trees,

my mind traces red and gold characters above door, wonders
what secret they hold; the proprietor names what he was
able to accomplish—call his own—in a land far from his birth.

Inside, a woman serves dim sum. She and I do not speak the same
language, so I blindly point at the carted food, hoping to select fish
or shrimp dumplings, and bypass what I suspect was taken from the
animals on display at the window.

I dismount steps to find vendor hovering over fruits.
Papaya he announces, the chilled air carrying the echo
of his thick accent, keeping it alive beyond my ears.

Star fruits call my love's name. On the return home, I hand
them to her as if a bouquet of flowers, "from Chinatown."

Japanese Folk Song

(for Thelonious Monk)

I

The city's name is printed
on my lips with ink.

Rubbed a thousand times
in falling snow.

Falling beneath the toy
created to play with.

Only if it dances to the
song that moves through

the radio. Through bones.
Through places where last was
seen everything now dead.

II

Call it Japanese Folk Song.

Call it everything but what it
actually is.

And life will belong to he
who bathes in the blood of the
innocent.

This scene came on a ship of
thoughts located on my legs.

Legs that move away from truth
and toward that which lies across
the opposite shore.

III

What is the meaning of this craft?

A friend told me he wants to give
up writing.

I told him to write.

Japanese Folk Song plays
when a toy is played with.

Before it breaks.
Before it falls to
pieces like human beings

exposed to the whims
of history.

School

They usher us into school like cows into pens. We chew information in
books and swallow ignorance in order to be enlightened. They brand us

Liberal Arts, Ivy League, State, City, Community, Public, Private, and we play
the part: minor and major. We were cool about school even though we did

not invent the rules. At the end of the time spent studying, we knew much
about who did what and what did what. But we knew nothing of ourselves,

of our history. We became blighted geniuses and sought ways to shed the
weight of the burden that came with the realization of being duped instead

of educated. We read books about revolutions and resistance movements: local,
global, and historical. We bypassed Mao and ran into Che. King was too much

like Gandhi, so we stuck with Malcolm. We bled anger and were not afraid of the
consequences of standing up to the system. Some of us were killed, put in prison,

self-destroyed, and some survived to keep the fight alive.

Mogadishu

I

Boys with rifles
bring terror to people,
see everyone the enemy
&
believe that alcohol and drugs
can kill fear.

II

They arrive bearing machines
stained with tears of gods.

> **Alchemy**
> On the day humans
> formed irons with their
> hands, the gods cried
> *look what they have done!*
> with bowed heads.

III

A boy was snatched on
the way to school.
Another rose from the
blood of his murdered father, mother,
and sister to join the rebels.

> **Dove**
> Missing the warmth of
> a familiar bed, an impatient
> Noah let out a dove from the
> Ark. It drowned; unable to
> fly above the flood.

IV

These are the child soldiers, says the
woman.

A priest kisses their cheeks, tasting salt
and more than a life-time of misery.

None would join the monastery. Amnesty
shipped them to the heartland of America
where they wait tables, lift bags, and
practice English by answering questions.
No, sir. We are not South Africans.

This Land

This land is rife with
tyranny.

This land was given
birth in unholy matrimony.

This land is not for me,
is not for you.

What are we doing
here?

Let us rebel; spit anarchy
from our mouths.

And create a revolution
that we'd not only talk
about.

Ichthys

Miles Smiles, I Smile

(for Miles Davis)

Miles is the man.
Miles is my man.
Miles is that man
who is my man.

Miles Smiles.
        All else is footnote to music.

Miles comes down like sun
on spine on back.

He breathes strength and joy
and instinct to destroy and build,
simultaneously.

Miles is the man.
My man Miles.

He hits the note.
Not sweet.
Not good.
Not bad.
        But all between and more.

Let me say here and anywhere that
when Miles Smiles, I smile.

The Cook

She rubs crushed ginger into rice frying
in a wok, first step of the recipe.

She follows orders when standing over a hot stove,
mind on stomach and its need to touch what must

first come from the Earth. She breathes love into
what she cooks, mixes vegetables above the heat;

watches them bend likes knees in prayer, not knowing
if life is sucked out or added to them. The final step calls

for soy sauce and ground pepper. The verdict will soon
come, mouths sit ready at a table passed down through

generations like the recipe she knows to perfection.

Above-Ground Movement

Fantasy
Red shoes with heel plant themselves
in bare back, grow vines across spine, and
wrap eternity in a hold too strong to disentangle.

Storyteller
My lover describes the force called love with eyes
that tell stories without end, no final page to say
this is where we stop or begin anew.

Skyscraper
Human and machine at play with steel. This is what
happens when we take the story of Babel literally.

Dream Catcher
I bring dreams with me. One is a bird unaware of
its ability to pollinate distant lands.

Music Paradise or When the Blues Man Overstays his Visit

I

>Saxophone

Long ago, the story goes, a man and a woman
ate a fruit and made music: A child with the

bluest eyes and the darkest skin that sang the
blues with eyes closed.

II

>Piano

So Cain and Abel were two dudes,
brothers.

Abel killed Cain because Cain slept with
his girl, Eve.

No. Eve was the mother.

Abel killed Cain.
Definitely.

III

>Trumpet

I walked to a house without door.
People sat on blocks of ice.

The sun was shining.

"Hey man, where you going?" a man yelled.

He was fat and wore a mean look on his face.
A look that said he can beat you—beat you
bad—just because he can.

I ran to him.
He held me by the throat with hands
of ropes and said, "hello."

IV

      Drums
Hands unable to stand still; always
hitting something.

Worn out mama's mahogany coffee table
with fingers that would strangle a man dead
and caress the softest parts of a woman's
body in a single motion.

V

      Guitar
Name's Robert Johnson.

I took what the devil gave me at the
crossroad to Dockery.

Life Together in Seven Steps

Courting
The day I talked to her, she said,
"boy, leave me alone."

But I talked until her smile
buried me in her life for years
to come.

She holding on to me like the scent
of sweat on a washed blouse.

I holding on to her because I do not
know how to let go.

Courting can be what it was not meant
to be, a thing other than a game,
competition without end.

Marriage
When the dove flew from the cage, my
nephew ran after them—hands outstretched,
mimicking the birds in flight.

Moments prior, the priest offered a sweet
soliloquy, "for better or worse."

The birds raced toward the setting sun.
Whatever light was left from the day's work
swallowed them.

Knowledge
I carried Jr. in my arms like a special jewel.
He taught me that something beyond the ordinary
lives in the ordinary.

I always wanted to be a good father, not having
sat at the feet of my father to learn the role
of fatherhood.

The knowledge that I came to, that came to me,
was not born in books but flowered on the vine
of experience.

    Wisdom
A still tongue keeps a wise head,
mother would say as I sat on her knees
learning more than religion.

I learned to bite my tongue but sometimes
it is a consuming fire, and there are times
when grief silences it.

    Dissolution
I too saw the doves leap head-first
into the setting sun.

I think of them when I hear
the screams of Jr. at night.

Screams that outlived him
and were first heard that day
I left him alone in the bath

for seconds that turned into eternity.

I see him, and the doves,
disappear into the setting sun.

Forgiveness
It was an accident, the doctors say.
But I know that mothers do not make
the kind of mistake I made.

Nothing—automobile, disease, insanity—
served as accomplice.
        I am to blame.
        Am blamed.
        I blame me.
        Blame is me.
And remain un-forgiven until I know
how to forgive me.

Love
She left a note about wanting to get away.
I waited for her to return and when she
returned, I received her with love.

Pyramidian

(after the sculpture by Mark Di Suvero)

Mathematician's cave.
Place where Earth makes love to self

wearing a garment of solace.

Pendulum swings, time stands still.

In you a hand holds another and
two hearts are one.

Mingus 'Ah Um

(for Charles Mingus)

Ride the waves with strings of bass.
Sounds too have names.

But the face-less, well, she stands at
the corner of this and that world waiting

for Mingus, he who plays with thunder
and strikes with lightning.

'Ah um is all he is.
All he is is 'ah um.

More than she can afford.

Isn't life funny? One day laughing, the
next crying.

Music knows this as humans know their
nature if only they confront it.

Mingus 'ah um comes from the gutter
where blood spills in sacrifice to the will
bound to life and its ways of being and not
being.

So too I cry.
So too I die,
unto self in this grave of soil and toil
and tomorrows.

Ichthys

I

I am left without the sea to beg relief.
        Gone are the days when rainbows filled
the sky of my heart.
        Today a bird
flew away without song.
        Lonely is the road that
leads to home; empty is my home.

II

I stand away from everything
        that is joyful.
        &
        Know
        what it means
        to stare beyond
        the past, searching
        for simplicity in being
        me.

III

But I digress.
Here is the dilemma:
How can one call
what is to be
into form?
The answer lives
in the steps taken
before the Fall
when humans
spoke with God
and all mysteries were
known.

Acknowledgements

I remain grateful toward the editors of the following publications for publishing my work.

"On Visit to Hellshire Beach (Jamaica)": *Lowestoft Chronicle*

"Amongst My African Brothers in NYC": *On the Rusk*

"Men Drinking, Boys Tormenting, Dogs Barking, Music Paradise or When the Blues Man Overstays His Visit": *Good Men Project*

"Epiphany": *The Guide Book*

"Vizcaya": *The Applicant*

"Nineveh": *Sojourners Magazine*

"Three Legged Buddha": *Inspired by My Museum Anthology* (Sampad Publishing)

"Black Moses": *Four Chambers Magazine*

"Samantha": *Chorus/Verse Anthology* (Jammi Publishing)

Notes

In On Visit to Hellshire Beach (Jamaica), bammie refers to fritters made of cassava.

The title My Mother Cried the Night She Fell Out of Love With Karl Malone was inspired by the song The Night Chicago Died by the group Paper Lace.

The line "But let me die fighting back" in Blackfish comes from the anti-lynching poem If We Must Die by Claude McKay. Mckay writes, "Like men we'll face the murderous, cowardly pack, pressed to the wall, dying, but fighting back."

Abeng in Someday My Prince Will Come is the carved horn of a cow or ram that marooned black slaves used to communicate with each other, blowing it at the start of a battle or when danger was in sight. The poem also references the song by Miles Davis.

Marcus Garvey encouraged black people world-wide, "up, you mighty race." I reinterpret this saying to "rise mighty warriors" in the poem Eschatology.

The title Black is the Color of my Hair comes from Black is the Color of My True Love's Hair by Nina Simone.

Samantha is a character in John Edgar Wideman's Sent for You Yesterday, a book in his Homewood Trilogy.

Several lines from the song Obeah Women by Nina Simone are in the poem of the same name, including the refrain "How do you think I lasted so long?"

"I beg you, dig me a hole to China. Or Africa." in the poem Streets of Missouri is drawn from Comment #1 by Gil Scott Heron, "After all is said and done, build a new route to China if they'll have you."

ELVIS ALVES was born in Guyana and raised in Brooklyn, New York. He is a graduate of Colgate University and Princeton Theological Seminary. Elvis's poetry has appeared in several magazines and journals, including *Poetry*, *Transition*, *Sojourners*, and *StepAway Magazine*. Elvis is the author of *Bitter Melon* (2013), *Ota Benga* (2017), *I Am No Battlefield But A Forest Of Trees Growing* (2018), winner of the Jacopone da Todi poetry book prize, sponsored by Franciscan University, Steubenville, Ohio (US), and *Black/White: We Are Not Panic (Pandemic) Free* (2020). Elvis lives in New York City with his family.

salmonpoetry

Cliffs of Moher, County Clare, Ireland

"Publishing the finest Irish and international literature."
Michael D. Higgins, President of Ireland